Random Thoughts

I hope you enjoy,

D. Henderson

Follow D. Henderson

Instagram: @d.henderson3488

Facebook: Darren J. Henderson

Library of Congress Cataloging-in-Publication Data

Register: 1-6770336201

Copyright 2018

Cover design by: Mr. Najji Wells

All rights reserved, including the right to reproduce this or portions thereof in any form whatsoever.

(1.)

Every night, immediately after saying my prayers I take a moment to reflect on my day's events. In my quest to become a better person, a more complete and compassionate man I search for moments I could have been kinder or more helpful. I find my joy everlasting when I give rather than receive; when I help instead of hinder. Every day I read and write, every day I learn something new, every day I share my findings with my family and friends in hopes of providing a deeper understanding of life and the challenges we face on a daily basis.

(2.)

You think you know me but you really don't. The only two people I need in my life are God and my Mama. The older I get the more comfortable I become within myself. I appreciate the quiet moments; the moments when it's just me and my thoughts, surrounded by soft jazz, and a dim light shimmering from the fireplace.

(3.)

I'm a private individual that spends a great deal of time reading and writing. I'm always in search of a new challenge, something that will entice, enlighten, and educate all in one. I'm passionate about many things, but nothing can compare to the love I feel for God and Family.

(4.)

I could trust a woman that I don't love, but I could never love a woman who I can't trust.

(5.)

I don't love this world; I love the people that cultivate it.

(6.)

Man makes money, money don't make a man. I speak from experience that having money doesn't guarantee happiness. One of the happiest moments of my life was when I was a freshman in college, my girl and I shared a cold-water flat off campus. Fine wining and dining consisted of a Big Mac, a large order of fries, and a coke with two straws. Like most college students, financially we were barely getting by, but we were high on love. There was nothing I enjoyed more in life than hugging and kissing her. I was addicted to her smile, her laughter, her kiss, her presence, I just couldn't get enough of her. When I say the best things in life are free, now you know what I'm talking about.

(7.)

The best job in the world is to get paid to do something that you love doing. That's a gift from God.

(8.)

There have been times when we've all said if I knew then what I know now I would have done things differently. That's a sign of growth. Only a fool refuses to acknowledge the error of past behavior. Whenever you encounter someone stuck on stupid keep moving.

(9.)

It is a huge difference between easy and a go-getter making the hard things look easy.

(10.)

The worse curse in the world is for a man to get comfortable being poverty-stricken; broke and lazy is the worst possible condition a man can find himself in. Once that sets in he becomes a professional beggar and a burden on his loved ones.

(11.)

A gangster with a conscious is like a pit bull with no teeth. All bark with no bite.

(12.)

When life is good we have a tendency to forget the promises we made in our darkest times.

(13.)

If he looks like a donkey, talks like a donkey, and acts like a donkey, he's a Jackass; what else do you need to know?

(14.)

Be careful what you wish for. Sometimes you can pursue something your entire life, obtain it and then discover that it's not what you really want.

(15.)

Growing up I played sports year-round, and when my team needed to raise funds we washed cars or sold tickets to a community function that we were hosting. It bothers me when I see a Coach sitting under a shaded tree at the intersection while his team is running up on cars begging for money, and we wonder why kids are so lazy.

(16.)

I find life more peaceful with less stress by doing the right thing every time, regardless of how it affects me or those I care about.

(17.)

The strongest commitment on earth should be between you and your God; followed by a Man and Wife. I'm strong on commitments; my character can be measured by my word. If I'm in a relationship my eyes don't wander, nor can I be distracted by a thin waist and pretty face. I believe it's a man's duty to protect his woman from emotional and physical pain. Infidelity cuts deeper than a knife and leaves a wound that may never heal.

(18.)

Those that know me know I'm strong minded and opinionated. Only science and facts can move me off my position; anything less is a waste of time.

(19.)

I've been to Hell and back; played poker with the Devil and won. Now I'm righteous, I don't value anything I can't take to the afterlife. My number one objective in life is to be on the right side of God when I close my eyes for the last time.

(20.)

When I confront ignorance I don't get mad I get sad. Some people just don't know better.

(21.)

Change always starts with the man in the mirror; the most amazing part about positive change is that everyone will notice it before you do.

(22.)

I support all talents and aspiration; Science as well as Arts, but there will come a time young people when you have got to get a JOB.

(23.)

In my closet, I have over 70 suits and 20 pairs of Alligator shoes, all of which represent the man I use to be. When I arrive at a family function I always show up in my work uniform which represents the man I am today. It hurts my heart when I hear my younger cousins reminiscing on the man I use to be. "Back in the days, Big Cuz had it going on; big houses, big cars, big money." The excitement I hear in their voices, the joy I witness in their eyes cuts me deeper than a knife. The realization that my past misdeeds have negatively affected those I care about only makes me strive harder, preach longer in my quest to make them understand that in order to survive in this world you must work; anything less, it's just a matter of time before you come up short.

(24.)

We live in a world of givers and takers, and the fact of the matter is those that give the most receive the least and those that give the least always expect the most.

(25.)

If your girl catches you cheating and smashes someone else you should get married; you two were meant to be together. A real lady would never stoop that low; she would shake you and keep moving.

(26.)

I know several cats that brag that they've never been to jail; the reason being is that they only violate members of their own family.

(27.)

Well rested and full of energy; I can see it but can't touch it. I'm close but still, have a little distance to go. I keep a pen and paper on the side of my bed in the event a brainstorm shakes me from my sleep. I pay attention to everything, ignoring no one. With high intensity, I move with a sense of urgency. There is nothing easy about life, especially when you're chasing new challenges. The pursuit of prosperity is a never-ending endeavor.

(28.)

When a boy becomes a man, he puts away childish things. Married with kids, at what age do you quit hanging out with the fellas?

(29.)

I still play by old-school rules; if you don't have something positive to say, please be quiet.

(30.)

Stop buying your kids what you've never had and start teaching them what you never knew. I've always believed education begins at home, and that strength of character; can only be bestowed by one's parents.

(31.)

Unprotected sex with porn stars, strippers, and prostitutes; word of advice Melania Trump "Go get tested."

(32.)

Time management is oh so important. It's a delicate balance between work and tending to the needs of one's family. In order to win you must capitalize on the moment; opportunities today may not exist tomorrow. Nothing in life worth having comes easy, the sacrifice always comes before the reward.

(33.)

The greatest treasure in life is happiness; which is a gift one can only receive through the blessings of God.

(34.)

I surround myself with God-fearing, hardworking people that keep me grounded and on top of my game. How can I lose?

(35.)

In order to understand other's, you must first understand who you are. In order to understand where you're going, you must understand where you came from. Growing up I bumped heads with my step-father on many occasions, and it wasn't until I was well into my twenties that we developed an understanding of each other. In an effort to understand how I, a star running back, Blue Ribbon wrestler, and Boy Scout could venture so far on the dark side of life, I approached my Pops searching for answers. After a moment of reflection he informed me growing up I was hard headed and refused to listen. I told him that if his style of teaching worked on my brothers; and didn't work on me he should have switched up his style, instead of giving up and allowing me to learn the hard way. I wasn't looking for fault, just a few answers that would give me a better understanding of my reckless behavior. Had we had this conversation sooner only God knows how much pain and heartache I could have avoided by making better decisions?

(36.)

It is not written in stone that all siblings must get alone, some must be loved from a distance.

(37.)

I know it may appear at times that I lack patience, and that I'm insensitive; it's only because I saw that movie before.

(38.)

There comes a time in one's life when you stop living for yourself and start living for others. I've reached that point. I compliment and admire the strong; but I gravitate towards those that need assistance, those that have everything they need to make it except the opportunity. I love to help, make a difference, and be a positive influence in someone's life. When I'm long gone, when someone thinks of me, I want them to remember me as being a good man, a hardworking, honest man. That's important to me.

(39.)

I love being surrounded by happy people. The sound of laughter, tears of joy, everyone feeling goofy.

(40.)

I support all family and friends and receive enormous joy in their accomplishments. Happy moments are meant to share.

(41.)

I'm a good listener, but I don't place a lot of emphasis on words. The mouth conveys whatever the mind instructs it to. A person's action reveals far more than their words. I know who loves me and who don't; I can see it in your eyes, and I can feel it in their touch.

(42.)

Dreams take form inside your mind but should be pursued with your heart. Whenever your heart and mind are aligned, it's hard to lose.

(43.)

The objective is not to drown; stay afloat, catch your breath, and swim again. Life is a marathon, not a sprint. Everybody won't make it to the end.

(44.)

The Devil is constantly trying to corrupt man with promises of quick riches. Only a weak hearted, weak minded man will fall for the weakest shit.

(45.)

2016 felt like I had the weight of the world resting on my shoulders. I knew absolutely too many people that were unemployed.

(46.)

There is so much suffering in this world that it's hard to enjoy moments of happiness. The Devil stays busy.

(47.)

You say you're tired. Aren't we all? You say you can't catch a break; now you're looking for a helping hand. If life doesn't go the way you plan, your planning is off track. The only way you can do better, you've got to know better.

(48.)

Family, what else can I say? Can't live with them, and can't live without them. Some cause you the greatest joy while others cause the greatest pain.

(49.)

A wise man once said: As time changes so do people, situations, and circumstances. Nothing in life remains the same; either people grow together or grow apart.

(50.)

Two strong minds will always bump heads, that's a healthy competition. We all can learn from each other; good conversation travels a long way.

(51.)

Making the right investment is the key to life. I don't invest in things I invest in people, more importantly in my woman. We're living in a time where it takes one to make it and two to win. In spite of my greatest efforts, there are times when I slip on a detail or two; and most times baby girl catches it for me. My girl brings a new and fresh perspective; I respect her mind. It's a sheer joy to be able to work and play with my best friend.

(52.)

There are moments like now when I feel happy for no apparent reason. It's a beautiful feeling, one that I truly cherish because it doesn't last long.

(53.)

Grown men acting like small children, and getting away with it? Can't stay young forever; eventually, you got to grow up. The baby needs his diapers changed.

(54.)

There was a time in my life when I said I was going to smoke weed until the day I die. That was before random drug testing. If smoking weed is more important than providing for your family, do your thing, keep smoking.

(55.)

Having a difference of opinion is okay; it's when you try to force your beliefs on others is where the problem comes in.

(56.)

Patience is a virtue; good things comes to those that wait, but not those that wait too long. Everything in life has an expiration date.

(57.)

Beauty is in the eye of the beholder and derives from a person's heart. Beyonce is pretty, Michelle Obama is beautiful. Halle Berry is pretty, Angela Davis is beautiful. I'll choose beauty over pretty every day of the week, and twice on Sunday.

(58.)

When my elders speak, I keep quiet and pay attention. That's called respect.

(59.)

In my life, I've been fortunate and unfortunate to cross paths with many people. Regardless of the image they project, I still believe there is some good in all people. Even the hardest heart can be tamed.

(60.)

Anytime you don't have time for yourself; you're spending too much time on others.

(61.)

I can't befriend anyone that doesn't respect their mother. If you don't care about her, you're incapable of caring about anyone. I don't understand how anyone can frown down on the woman that gave them life. She might not have been the perfect mother, but were you the perfect child? If you can't forgive her, who can you forgive?

(62.)

The right spouse will bring out your best; elevate you to heights you've only dreamed about. The wrong spouse will keep you in the gutter; hold you down like a pair of cement boots.

(63.)

A good deal is when everyone walks away happy.

(64.)

I don't chase money; I chase dreams. Man makes money; money doesn't make a man. I don't put material possessions before my people. All the money in the world means nothing if you don't have anyone to share it with.

(65.)

It is sad when people close to you are slick-side hating. Misery is contagious like the flu, the closer you come in contact, the better the odds of you catching it.

(66.)

I'm a man with many flaws and gifts. One of my greatest gifts is my ability to communicate with all walks of life. In my darkest times, I used writing as a mechanism to escape the madness associated with everyday life. Life lessons are sometimes hard and often brutal. There are certain mistakes you make you simply can't recover from. Think before you act.

(67.)

Black, white, brown or yellow we're all God's creatures and share the same basic characteristics. Sit down, let's talk, we've got to have something in common.

(68.)

The best things in life are often discovered when you're not looking.

(69.)

Sometimes God blesses a person with all the material possessions their heart desire, just to show you money doesn't equal happiness. The more money, the more problems!

(70.)

The best feeling in the world is to love and be loved in return.

(71.)

I can't wait for the New Year to hit. New job, new look, new resolutions. Out with the old and in with the new. I'm about to make some serious changes if you don't hear from me after the first you're one of those changes.

(72.)

Living in the moment life never felt so beautiful; happy like a child chasing butterflies, a child can't see past next week, that's why he lives each day to the fullest.

(73.)

It was a long hard journey to get to this point. I don't take this hustle for granted and appreciate all the fruit it bears. Money determines many things, like Hamburger v. Steak, Motel 6 v. The Four Seasons, Public School v. Private School. Money doesn't make you happy but it damn sure makes a difference.

(74.)

Surviving Compton...Dr. Dre made Ike Turner look like a saint. Monsters come in all colors.

(75.)

Anytime a man can't look you in the eyes when he's talking, he's being deceptive. It's hard to fake sincerity, because the eyes don't lie.

(76.)

Right now is a time for reflection, 2017 was awesome, a spectacular year filled with many wonderful gifts. From start to finish, professional, as well as personal blessings, came in abundance. I know I shouldn't, but I must give thanks to my haters and naysayers whom I received much energy, and a great deal of motivation. Thank you.

(77.)

I don't entertain Race base excuses, shut it down immediately. My people don't need a head start; just give them a fair start.

(78.)

There are a lot of subjects I don't speak on out of respect for those that think otherwise. It's okay to agree to disagree.

(79.)

A man's worth is measured by his word. The only thing you owe mankind is the truth. To say you will with no intentions of staying true; means you're hindering instead of helping. Quit faking!

(80.)

Tomorrow is not promised; you've got to live every day like it's your last.

(81.)

You're a cheater; she's a cheater. What's the problem? I thought they call that an open relationship.

(82.)

Stupidity is when you do dumb shit without thinking, and the first thing fly out your mouth is "My bad." Really?

(83.)

No job, no money, no car and you snuck inside the club. Exactly who are you looking for?

(84.)

If everything goes as planned, grab a bag of popcorn and a front row seat and watch this come up.

(85.)

I realize old habits die hard, that's why I show so much patience and understanding when I'm dealing with the younger generation. They claim to be hard but some are sensitive like girls. Come too hard, talk too slick they might feel played. I don't care how tough they think they are when you come around here you will pull up your pants and refrain from using the N-word.

(86.)

If you enjoy playing, be a player; but don't play while in a committed relationship. Stay single and do your thing.

(87.)

New Year Day has always been grade time; the day I calculate my wins and losses. If you have less January 2018 than you had January 2017, something went wrong.

(88.)

Kids do what they see, and repeat what they hear. If you want them to tighten up their behavior then tighten up yours.

(89.)

My understanding of life is far from complete. I read to achieve a greater understanding of life and people. I try my hardest not to be judgmental, how can I frown upon another when I, myself have not lived an honorable life. We all have a story to tell, some a little bit sadder than others. We live, we learn, we push forward.

(90.)

Most people lie when scared or in trouble; then you have people that lie for no apparent reason whatsoever. You don't have to lie to kick it.

(91.)

Chasing paper is a Thinking Man's game, where the size of your bankroll determines how you live.

(92.)

Marriage is a covenant between Man, Woman, and God. If you commit adultery, you have officially broken your vows. In God's eyes, you're no longer married. Your marriage certificate is reduced to a piece of paper you can wipe your ass with it.

(93.)

God didn't create man to live in captivity, but I do understand when you act like an animal society has a right to treat you like one.

(94.)

Spreading rumors is worse than starting them. It doesn't cost a dime to mind your business.

(95.)

Hard work is a trait everyone recognizes and respect.

(96.)

Social Media has provided many blessings. Not only has it provided the opportunity to reunite and stay in touch with family and friends, but it has also provided the opportunity to meet many wonderful people. As in all things in life, there's a flip side. As sad as it is Social Media has also broken up marriages, turned best friends into enemies, and created a platform to broadcast people at their worse. Be careful what you post because once you send it, there's no getting it back.

(97.)

Every day you wake up is the first day of the rest of your life.

(98.)

I chase what my heart desires; sometimes the chase is just as fulfilling as the capture.

(99.)

The only thing I fear in life is being broke. The mere thought of not having the means to provide for my family scares the shit out of me; and that my friend is why I work so hard.

(100.)

Time management is oh so important in maintaining a healthy, balanced life.

(101.)

I'm respectful, but far from friendly. I enjoy being in the company of positive people. I would love to know how you're doing, only if you're doing well. I'm not one you come to vent. I'm really not trying to entertain no one else problems; I've got enough of my own.

(102.)

I would be the first to admit some women have done an excellent job raising a male child, but I still believe it takes a man to train a boy how to be a man. I never met a boy who said his mother taught him how to fight, fish, hunt, or survive in the mountains if he got lost.

(103.)

I recognize and abide by laws written by man; it is the laws handed down by God I govern my life by.

(104.)

I'd rather give a homeless person a hundred dollars, than give someone I know ten dollars to go gamble with.

(105.)

I've reached the point in life where I don't have time for senseless conversation. If I tell you grass is green and you tell me; no it's not, its olive. Bye, that's the end of the conversation.

(106.)

What's obvious to most sometimes is oblivious to others; the mind is a terrible thing to waste. Just say No to drugs.

(107.)

There are days like now when I ask myself what's keeping me in the Big Easy? Hot and humid in the summer; cold and wet in the winter, and hurricanes that are becoming more deadly and destructive each year; then I think about my Mama, and it all makes sense. Home is where the heart is at.

(108.)

I know some people who believe going to church on Sunday forgives six days of sinful living. Do your thing Lil Daddy; I'm not mad at you.

(109.)

I love the sunshine, but I'm at my best when it rains. Never one to cry over spilled milk when all I got to do is wipe it up; complaining about life's problems only hinder your ability to solve them.

(110.)

Some of the most dishonest people I've ever met never been to jail, and some of the realist people that I know took a trip up north and back. It does not matter where you've been; it's about where you're at, at this moment in your life.

(111.)

I'm not a kid in the candy store; I don't need to sample everything that appears sweet. I'm a grown man now I know exactly what I'm looking for.

(112.)

The most beautiful feeling in the world is true love; to love and be loved completely.

(113.)

Life is not meant to live alone, nor is it meant to be shared with someone that's not right for you. As in all relationships; either you grow together or you grow apart, nothing in life remains the same. The day you stop talking is the day you can officially call it quits.

(114.)

Sometimes smart people do dumb things, like loaning money to someone that doesn't have a job; then get mad when they can't pay you back.

(115.)

In spite of all the ugliness on this planet I believe in the goodness of all mankind. I believe there are far more good-hearted people than there are evil people, and good always prevails over evil.

(116.)

I've made many mistakes in my life; I can write a book on what not to do.

(117.)

All relationships don't lead to marriage; all marriages don't last forever. If it must end, make sure the woman is in a better position leaving than she was in when she arrived.

(118.)

My heart aches and tears burn my eyes when I think of the ill-deeds I committed against mankind. Only the Lord knows the depth of my sorrow, and only the Lord can judge me before he lays me to rest. How many times can a man apologize?

(119.)

True love always shines the brightest in your darkest moments.

(120.)

The higher I climb; the easier it is to spot the wolves dressed in sheep clothing. Crooked eyes always follow fake smiles. They wish you well; and at the same time be slick-side hating. "Keep your friends close, and keep your enemies even closer." I always believed that to be a flawed concept. If you play with snakes; eventually you will get bitten. Bear in mind; some bites are more poisonous than others, you might not recover.

(121.)

Do you know why you don't find a lot of college educated people in prison? They're too smart to break the law. Ignorance always appears to make a lot of sense when you're speaking to a group of high school drop-outs.

(122.)

It's a parent's responsibility to provide for the child when they're young. It's the child's responsibility to provide for the parent when they get old. It's quite simple, what's the problem?

(123.)

People associate having money with being smart. I beg to differ; some of the riches people do the dumbest shit.

(124.)

Growing up my parents set the bar too low. As long as I got passing grades I was good. In hindsight that was the biggest mistake they made. Push your kids to their fullest potential; you never know you might have the next Obama sitting at your dining room table.

(125.)

I never was a sucker for a sad story because I believe very few men have been through the shit I been through, and survived to talk about it. Don't judge a book by the cover; you never know what's inside?

(126.)

If you stay ready you don't have to get ready. Opportunities today may not be there tomorrow. Early bird gets the worm; you got to capitalize on the moment.

(127.)

True Love by nature will make a cheater stop cheating, and a liar quit lying.

(128.)

Getting up in age; every day got to count. There's nothing more valuable than my time; I simply don't have any to waste. Please don't disturb my groove; share your joy and your happiness. Let's laugh.

(129.)

I've never been married; therefore I never give marital advice, but it never seems to amaze me when someone working on their third marriage is quick to do so. I have one child; therefore I don't believe I'm qualified to give parental advice, but it never seems to amaze me when someone with a pregnant 15-year-old daughter and a 13-year-old son in juvenile detention is quick to do so. Sometimes it's okay to keep your opinion to yourself;

rather than speak on something you obviously know little about.

(130.)

It's amazing how you can be around a person 25 years and don't know their birthday, favorite color, food, or music. You can only imagine what else you don't know about them. Don't be too quick to call someone a friend just because you have known them an X-amount of years.

(131.)

Happiness is not an illusion; it's obtainable, but first, you must rid yourself of everything and everyone that's causing you grief.

(132.)

2018 is upon us, never in my life have I ever been more focused, more serious, more determined. Trump said: "Black Lives don't Matter" and $7.25 an hour is too high. He promised more jobs at cheaper wages. Let the rich get richer, and let the poor die off and disappear.

(133.)

Tomorrow is not promised, it's only by the grace of God we're able to see another day. Every day I talk to my family and friends I tell them I love them; in the event I don't see them again. It's a heartfelt practice that I enjoy expressing.

(134.)

I love the pursuit of love, wining and dining that special lady. I love romancing her, holding her hand, opening her door, and pulling out her chair. I love the sound of her laughter, the look in her eyes when I surprise her with flowers, earrings, or a kiss when she least expects.

(135.)

Whenever in doubt I rely on my senses to guide me through troubled times; I always believed its God's way of communicating.

(136.)

At ten years old you're still a child curious about life. At twenty years old you're a young man that thinks you know everything.

At thirty years old you acknowledge you really don't know squat and start showing the first signs of adulthood. At forty years old, congratulations, you're now a man.

(137.)

Something is wrong; I can't imagine why a teen would tattoo a gun on his face. (Doomed for life) Or why these youngsters believe wearing their pants under the cheek of their ass is gangsta. (Indecent exposure) Where did we go wrong? SMH

(138.)

If the man I am today could meet the man I was twenty years ago, I would kick his ass.

(139.)

I've never been one to place unreasonable expectations on my family or friends, but lying is a trait I can't associate with.

(140.)

Every day you open your eyes you should count your blessings. Every day you laugh and smile you should be grateful. Every day you're able to help others you should be extremely thankful; sometimes the best blessings come in the form of a simple Thank You.

(141.)

The Mississippi River, a dark and dangerous place, the 5th largest river in the world with a current so strong it'll take the best swimmers under. There was a time when the dangers excited me; now that I'm a little older, much wiser I sense my days out here is coming to an end, and I'm good with that.

(142.)

I love a meeting of the minds, exchanging meaningful conversation, especially with a stranger; that's the foundation of a new friendship.

(143.)

I know what I'm looking for; I don't have to think about it twice.

(144.)

A lot of people fail to understand just because you love a person don't necessarily make that person love you. People are known to do silly things in pursuit of love; the harder they try the more desperate they look. If you got to go through all this to catch someone's attention, there's a strong possibility that might not be the right person for you.

(145.)

Fake friends and enemies are one and the same; they both despise you, they both love to see you fail, and they don't even know you. A hater doesn't need a reason to hate; they hate just because.

(146.)

Everyone loves a winner especially if they can borrow some cash. The moment you tell them no you're about to be all kinds of bitches. If your relationship is based on you giving all the time, you're being used.

(147.)

I'm a man that loves a challenge, and I often challenge my family and close friends. I challenge the kids to get straight A's, the teens to be more helpful to their parents, and the adults to live healthier, quit smoking, quit drinking and exercise more. We must challenge ourselves and our loved ones on the regular to bring out their very best.

(148.)

My trust comes with a handshake. It's not something you must earn, but it's something you can quickly lose. One of my greatest flaws is my inability to forgive those that wrong me; I'm working on it. Sometimes happiness can be acquired by not what you gain, but in what you let go.

(149.)

Only my closest family and friends know where I've been, but only God knows where I am going.

(150.)

There was a time when I didn't trust anyone but myself; a time when I was knee deep in bullshit and the best way to move was alone. After years of bumping my head against the wall, I was force to acknowledge I was headed down the wrong path. Unable to change my past and preserve my future, I surrendered to Almighty God. The best decision I ever made.

(151.)

People give in different ways; some write a check while others volunteer their time, I like to do both if I'm able. It's only by the grace of God I have the means to help. I give freely, without conditions; my blessings don't come from man, they come from God.

(152.)

Have you ever wondered why they hate us so much? Why is it so easy for law enforcement to manhandle our sisters, daughters, wives and mothers? I simply can't understand how a grown man can gun down an unarmed youth, regardless of race and not be severely affected by it? You just killed a kid; somebody's child. How do you sleep at night?

(153.)

Love is so powerful that you can recognize it by a mere glance. You can hear it in her voice; feel it in her touch. Love is so precious and fragile. You must handle it with care.

(154.)

I find it amusing how some people can smell everybody else's shit but can't smell their own. Imagine that?

(155.)

When the student becomes the teacher, the teacher becomes the student. You're never too old to learn, and you're never too young to teach.

(156.)

Having faith does not guarantee a trouble-free life; having faith does provide you with the strength to deal with anything life throw your way. To have faith is an unquestioning belief, through God anything is possible.

(157.)

I often tell my nephews what's pleasing to the eyes is sometimes heavy on the heart. I'd rather be smitten by a woman's mind rather than captivated by her rear-end. We're living in a time where you've got to be a power couple to meet the demands of a global economy. When it's time to make a move every able body in the house got to go somewhere; if not work than school, but you got to get out of here.

(158.)

Something is going on deep inside my soul; a joy so profound I wake up every morning with a smile on my face. Good things happen to good people, keep the faith.

(159.)

Never one to comment on someone's post; when I come across a post that moves me I usually share it, in hopes, it'll make someone else smile. When I come across a post that disturbs me; I immediately delete it and unfriend the sender.

(160.)

When I see a young brother's pants hanging under his ass, mean mugging, looking like he wants to kill somebody, the first thing comes to mind: A Thug needs a hug.

(161.)

Experience taught me time heals all wounds, emotional as well as physical. When all else fails; put it in God's hand and watch the miracle unfold.

(162.)

The holiday is over, but the memories are sure to last a lifetime. Only by the blessings of God I met the most amazing woman. What started off as innocent flirting, quickly took on a life of its own. I like her and I'm pretty sure baby is feeling me. It's going to be an interesting year.

(163.)

The child doesn't get to choose their parents, but the parents get to choose who they have a child by. Wrap it up!

(164.)

I don't answer unknown callers, nor do I open the door without checking the surveillance cameras. There is no price you can place on Peace of Mind. Coming from a big family has its perks, and it also has its disadvantages. More people, more problems. Everyone got a sad story to tell, one that'll bring you to tears if you didn't know better. Sometimes you got to duck and hide from your own kind.

(165.)

Everything that glitters is not gold; what's soothing to the eyes can be detrimental for the heart. Be careful what you wish for; sometimes a dream can turn into a nightmare. Instead of praying for wealth or material gain, pray for good health and happiness.

(166.)

I remember back in the days, if a kids got straight A's they were well behaved. Nowadays these kids get straight A's and are too smart for their own good.

(167.)

Key to success is to know what you want at a young age and pursuing it with every fiber inside you. Words without deeds are faking at its best. If you don't believe in yourself, why should I?

(168.)

My co-worker told me to slow down I was making him look bad. "No player you need to catch up, you're making yourself look bad."

(169.)

Every now and then I find myself trapped inside my own thoughts, trying to understand what makes me tick. Reflecting on the past doesn't always generate warm moments. To the contrary sometimes you're reminded of incidents you rather forget. Everyone has a few life embarrassing moments.

(170.)

I can deal with every kind of person on this planet except a liar, thief, cheater, and I'm also not fond of the lazy. The quickest way to lose my attention is to start complaining about life. If you don't like your conditions, change them.

(171.)

The hard part about maintaining a New Year's Resolution is it gets harder every day. My ability to be steadfast can be contributed to my refusal to fake on myself. My word is my bond, double important when I say it in silence.

(172.)

Trust in another is the foundation of a beautiful friendship. It's a beautiful feeling when you know you have some people you can really count on.

(173.)

Nothing in life worth having comes easy. The more you want; the more you must risk. If you want it all, you must be willing to lose it all.

(174.)

I realize no one is perfect, and mistakes will be made. The best part about messing up is asking for forgiveness and becoming a wiser and better person.

(175.)

I'm a red-blooded African American man, and I do appreciate the sight of a beautiful derriere, but I must admit I often wonder if there any substance with a woman who believes she must show her backside every time she takes a picture?

(176.)

Never one to turn my back on a friend, especially in times of need; I've been told I'm loyal to a fault? Perhaps I am. I choose my friends carefully, love em like my family. Our understanding is complete; we play it like grown folks. If by plan or accident one of my friends involve me in some bullshit, that's the day we stop being friends.

(177.)

I treat others the same way I want to be treated, and that's with the utmost respect.

(178.)

I remember when I was a child I loved watching my mother dance to Blue Magic, the Temptations, Smokey, and Aretha. I can only imagine what my vocabulary would have been like had I grown up on Gangsta's Rap.

(179.)

I'm somewhat optimistic about the future; I do have my reservations. Global perception of the USA has shifted, people are speaking their minds, and it's not nice. I don't have a clue how this is going to turn out?

(180.)

Last night was one of those nights I wish I would've stayed home. It was so cold I couldn't feel my finger-tips, toes, or my nose. Heavy rain, strong winds, and chilling temperatures are an ugly and dangerous combination on the river. I can't deny it; I use to love it, and it made me feel alive; now it's unfulfilling and a little scary.

(181.)

Bad news and sad news equals mental anguish. Talking to some people is just as exhausting as 10 hours of hard labor.

(182.)

I always believed everyone deserves forgiveness, especially family; but I also feel it's hard to forgive someone that has never apologized.

(183.)

I often share long conversation with my friends. I like to know about the people I hang with and bring around my family. It would be wonderful if all my friends were friends.

(184.)

I smile when I think of a woman, how can I not? I realize everyone is not blessed with that special someone, and to some it's hard to visualize something you can't imagine. Her smile is so alluring the mere sight of her is enough to chase her to the end of earth. God couldn't have designed a more beautiful companion for man. A woman is more precious than any stone the earth can produce;

if you treat her like a Queen she'll treat you like a King.

(185.)

A fair exchange is not a robbery; read the small print before you sign.

(186.)

Most people believe a man and woman is incapable of being friends without a physical attraction. Some of my closest friends are women; women I've known for years. Friends don't tag friends; true friendship is too valuable to gamble with.

(187.)

My dude told me his new girl had a sweet tooth and he knew just what to get her for Valentine Day. Being that chocolate was her favorite candy, he decided to have a basket made with every kind of chocolate you could imagine. Armed with his video camera, he couldn't wait to capture the moment. He sat quietly as his girl opened the basket and dumped all the chocolate on the bed. "What's wrong?" He asked, after observing a gloomy look on face. "Where is the jewelry?" She shot back. "I can buy my own candy." I laughed so hard I fell out my chair.

(188.)

Peace of mind is the key to serenity, and wisdom is the key to understanding. I've never met anyone that didn't enjoy laughing. Why anyone would choose misery over joy is beyond my understanding. If I ever come across such a person; I will shake him so fast he'll be dizzy when he look back up.

(189.)

I'm a student of life, and I must learn something new every day. Every morning I wake up, make a stiff cup of coffee, press play and allow the sound of soft jazz to set the mood. Its 4am, the city is still sleeping; time to get it in.

(190.)

Everything doesn't deserve a response; sometimes your silence can be more effective than an outburst.

(191.)

I have a tendency to smile when I'm uncomfortable; it's a defense mechanism I employ while my mind is sizing up the situation. My first thought is to separate myself from the bullshit, by simply walking away, if the bullshit follows me than I got to check it. I realize there is no pleasant way to say the unpleasant, and there is no way to determine what type of reaction I may get; therefore I got to prepare for everything. Some people are hard to avoid, like a full-fledge bully, he picked the wrong one today.

(192.)

Expectations are the number one cause of disappointment. We expect people to play fair, be honest, and not lie. We expect our family and friends to be there when we need them. We expect the teachers to teach, and our children to learn. We expect our preachers to preach, and our spouse not to cheat; it would be fair to say we expect a lot.

(193.)

The higher you get, the fresher the air becomes which is evidence how corrupt and polluted the earth is. Satan comes with a stint that's hard to ignore. When you hear about a tragedy, the Devil is at work. He never sleeps; always searching for the right time, when you're at your weakest; to whisper in your ear and lead you down a path of destruction.

(194.)

I try to avoid all negative communications, illicit conversation about things that don't interest me. There is only one thing worse than no advice, and that's bad advice. Beware of those that know it all because usually, they don't know a damn thing.

(195.)

I know some people with buzzard's luck, couldn't win even if they cheated. If they say bet on red, than you should bet on black; in spite of their track record they keep gambling; losing everything from their life savings to their rent money, and swear up and down they don't have a problem.

(196.)

My whole life is based on my faith in God. It's the one thing I never question, and the first place I turn for guidance. I'm not perfect; far from it. Man makes mistake, he's only human. The mistake is not the sin, the intent is.

(197.)

My brother asked me why I work so hard and never buy anything. I told him the best things in life are free. I handed him the ball, "first one to ten wins, you got to win by two."

(198.)

I don't entertain the small and petty. Hold that thought; I'll get right back with you.

(199.)

I have known sadness; I've learned if you can't control it, it will consume you. If it's too heavy to carry; put it in God's hands.

(200.)

Failing does not define man it's how you bounce back that does. Everything in life has a purpose and a destiny. Never start something you can't finish.

(201.)

Life is about trials and tribulations, and the pursuit of happiness. The objectivity is not to win them all, but you must win the most.

(202.)

Everyday life presents something new, a new challenge, a new desire, a new hope, a new promise; and every day you must decide what to pursue and what to discard. Only you know what's important to you. You can't chase someone else's dreams.

(203.)

When I speak about life, love, and happiness; for the most part I'm speaking from past experience. By the grace of God I have known a love that had no boundaries. It's a love I'll never forget, one that I cherish with all my heart. The Lord said, only Love can replace Love. Hello Cathy.

(204.)

I'm a romantic at heart, I love holding my woman's hand, touching her, kissing her. Opening doors, and pulling out chairs is automatic, it goes without saying. If she's cold, I will gladly give her my coat, my shirt if need be. The same way I hold her down she holds me down. We share the same bed, it's only fitting we share the same name, the same bank account.

(205.)

When you say "I do" you're supposed to become one, mind, body, and soul. Where did it go wrong?

(206.)

I know it may appear at times that I'm talking about you, a complete stranger, someone I never met. As humans most of us share the same basic characteristics, wants, desires, dreams, and of course the same problems. What separates us is how we deal with these problems.

(207.)

If you're not happy at home; then you're most certainly not happy at work. How long can you sustain this level of discomfort? Sometimes you got to let it go.

(208.)

In my journey I had the enormous pleasure of meeting some beautiful couples; one sharing their 40-year marriage anniversary and the other sharing their 50-year anniversary. Only love can keep you together that long, to see it in the flesh only made it that much more special. I gladly paid for their meal, and quietly wondered where my special lady was?

(209.)

My friend said all couples fight. "No, they don't," I said, looking at the scratches on his face and neck. The moment it turns violent is the moment you leave it alone.

(210.)

How can you tell if she's the right one for you? When the sound of her laughter fills you with joy; when her smile dismantles all your defenses, and when you think about her all day.

(211.)

They say opposites attract; I disagree. I need a woman likeminded and on point, one that moves the way I move, straight ahead, never backward.

(212.)

There is nothing more frustrating than dealing with a hardhead youngster that thinks he knows it all. The amount of energy one must exhaust to get your point across will drain you. Not only will they ruin the moment they have a way of affecting the rest of your day. Beware of 'The Mood Killers' they're all around you.

(213.)

One of my New Year's Resolutions was to grind from the first day of the year to the last. I define Grind working 60-70 hours a week, every week for a year. Eight months in, my mind was sharp as a razor but my body began to show signs of fatigue. Determined like it was still January; I added another hour of sleep and P6, a testosterone booster to my diet. Sometimes you got make adjustments to get to where you're going.

(214.)

I usually have a backup plan for everything; she convinced me I didn't need one for her. I took her word, and I'm glad I did.

(215.)

A house always appears prettier on the outside than it does on the inside. Couples always seem happier in public than they do at home. People seem to believe happiness comes from material wealth; only the rich know otherwise. Sometimes what appears to be the American Dream turns out to be a nightmare plagued with alcohol, depression, and drug abuse?

(216.)

If a woman marries a man because he's a good provider, don't expect anything more, you've been bought. Don't complain when he's missing in action for three days; the bills are paid. Some men believe if they're the sole provider; they're entitled to do as they please. If you don't think something is wrong with cheating, you'll never stop. If marriage is based on anything besides love, it was doomed from the beginning.

(217.)

I like the man I've become; cooler than a spring breeze, a man's man that stands on everything right. I know what it takes to win. Hard work has never failed me.

(218.)

People are quick to judge, find fault in others; but can't stand up to the same scrutiny.

(219.)

There is nothing better than hands-on training. I'm a visual learner; if I see you do it one time I got you. I grew up believing anything a man can do I can do.

(220.)

If he looks like a donkey, walks like a donkey, acts like a donkey, he's a jack-ass; wishful thinking is not going to change him!

(221.)

I know some people are super cool when they're not drinking, but the sad part they drink every day. If you know a person can't handle their alcohol, why do you keep feeding him drinks, and get mad when he starts acting up?

(222.)

Some people are more tolerable than others, and some people will dismiss you so quick you won't remember the exchange. I love dealing with real people, my kind of people where I don't have to mimic my words. Never in my life have I ever encountered so many sensitive gangsters, harmless as a fly on the wall. They got the talking part of the game down to a science, but when it's time to put in work they can't be found.

(223.)

Looking back, all the signs were visible, clear as writing on the wall. You scratch your head wondering how you missed it. The brightest ideas today sometimes turn into the dumbest ideas tomorrow. Sometimes you must visualize what lies ahead and plan accordingly.

(224.)

I try my hardest to avoid bullshit, but sometimes I find myself caught right in the middle of it. Coming from a big family; it's hard to miss it. For the most part, it's a laughable moment; but on some occasions it does get a little sticky.

(225.)

I haven't left and I miss the city already. There is something very charming about the Big Easy. I love the cultural, the abundance of wisdom that can be found at every park and hanging in the front of every corner store. They all got a story to tell and I enjoy hearing it. I didn't realize how many wonderful people I came to know until it was time to say goodbye. It felt good knowing I gave just as well as I received.

(226.)

Sometimes life's greatest lessons come in your darkest times; when the weight of the world seems to be wearing you down. While the weak succumb to the pressure, the strong always fight past it. A wise man once said things are never so bad they can't get worse, and if you ever find yourself in a hole, the first thing you got to do is quit digging.

(227.)

I don't care if you don't have money, a car, or a job. There is nothing wrong with not having anything; there is definitely something wrong when a person doesn't want anything.

(228.)

Life without love is like an ocean without waves, a sky without stars, and a rainbow without colors. "Come here Lil Mama, don't cry, and dry your eyes. Love is never complicated; when you find a man that treats you better than your Daddy, that's the man you marry.

(229.)

What's a father you never met, a mother always with her hand out, a brother you can't rely on, and a sister you can't trust? A stranger on the streets!

(230.)

In order to find peace, you must first rid your life of everyone that's causing you grief.

(231.)

My father passed when I was two years old in an automobile accident, leaving my mother a widow at nineteen with two infants still in diapers. On days my mother couldn't find someone to watch me she'd take me to work with her. I can remember my mother scrubbing floors like it was yesterday. The struggle burns inside my mind like an inferno that will never go out. My number priority in life is to make my Mama's life as comfortable as possible. All she got to do is hint she want something, and I'm ma make it happen. They call me a Mama's boy; I'll wear that.

(232.)

These years are flying by; despite man's greatest efforts he can't stop the hands of time. There is so much I have yet to experience, a love I yearn to know, and places I have yet to travel. I'm not close to being finish; as long as I've got air in my lungs, I've got a life to live.

(233.)

Growing up on the wicked streets of Southeast I acquired street sense years before I learned book sense. The bigger the lick the harder the fall; point seen money gone; get in where you fit in. Everything isn't for everybody; confusion always comes before clarity.

(234.)

The next time you feel like judging someone, close your eyes and think about the skeletons in your closet. We all have some.

(235.)

You can make a person hate you; you can't make a person love you. You can make a person fear you; you can't make a person respect you. Be mindful of how you treat others.

(236.)

I come up in an era when a man's word was his bond; when all it took was a handshake to seal a deal. In 2018 faking is at an all-time high; a Lie don't care who tells it.

(237.)

The true definition of a female friend is someone you love like a sister, but she won't hesitate to check you like your mother.

(238.)

There is nothing I enjoy more than reading with my favorite music in the background. It's a pleasure that requires no company.

(239.)

I don't know how to mend a broken heart. I don't know how to counsel physical or emotional abuse. I don't know how to repair trust. I don't know how to make-up for everything your ex did to you. All I know is how to be me; a gentleman at all times.

(240.)

I hate when someone near and dear to my heart crosses me because I must suffer two loses; one from the cross and the second from a loss of trust.

(241.)

"It is easier to build strong boys; than it is to repair broken men." Fredrick Douglas.

(242.)

At some point in your life you must accept the inevitable; no one can live forever. Seriously who would want too? Eighty years on God's green earth should be enough, depending on one's health it might be too long. I have reached the point in life where the mere thought of residing in God's kingdom is truly a paradise I look forward to. Every time I open my eyes I greet the day with a smile, I feel blessed. It been a long, hard journey, but I finally made it. Thank you Lord.

(243.)

Reflecting on the past and questioning the future will lead to wiser decisions. Looking back I had to ask myself who on this earth cost me the greatest heartache? As sad as it was to acknowledge, I was forced to admit it was I, (as a result of years of bad decision making) the sole person responsible for causing me the most grief. When you take ownership of your failings, then and only then can you take the necessary steps needed to correct them.

(244.)

Memories of past failures burn inside my mind like an everlasting torch. I welcome it because it's a constant reminder of everything I've been through and how far I came. There is not a soul on earth that hasn't experience hard times, but unlike most, I turn stress into energy. Every challenge I encounter I give my all. Win, lose, or draw will never be determined by a lack of effort.

(245.)

I'm constantly moving pieces, seeing what works and what don't. Life is about making adjustments, stopping on a dime and coming with something new.

(246.)

I never been one to roll with a crowd. If we're cool, I'll meet you there. I sport a two seater now, just enough room for me and my girl.

(247.)

Waiting for someone to give you something, you'll never have anything.

(248.)

There was a time when I could spot bullshit with a mere glance, now I got to take a double look, and I still might be wrong. I've come to learn you don't have to be a gangster to be corrupt, or a street-walker to be a hoe; there is a whole society of the working class people who are on some dirty, low-down shit. Protect yourself at all times.

(249.)

I hate when people take something pretty and make it ugly; take something innocent and make it guilty. I hate when people allow past doubts and insecurities to complicate future growth. Some people are so afraid of losing that special someone they do everything in their power to run em off. It's hard to be right with someone else when you're not right with yourself.

(250.)

I often wondered why some people feel the need to impress those that care very little about them? Ass-kissing and boot-licking might get you a raise, but it will never buy you respect; and it's hard to lead men that don't respect you.

(251.)

There is no need to negotiate I've come too far to compromise, and I'm too old to take shorts. I lost count how many times I got it wrong before I got it right. How many opportunities came and went before I started capitalizing on them. In spite of my many failings, I never lost faith and I never gave up. A winner never quits, a quitter never wins.

(252.)

I have been blessed with a beautiful woman, a nice job, a nice house, and a nice car. I'm not rich, but I'm far from being broke. If it was about me, I could sit back, kick off my shoes and coast the rest of the way. But it's not about me; it's about everyone that's near and dear to me, and providing them with the means necessary to chase their dreams. The Dynasty must start somewhere, why not with me?

(253.)

I don't believe there's an individual on this earth God didn't bless with a talent. Some people go their entire life without discovering the talent that lies inside, while others recognized but never capitalize on it. Singing in the shower to an audience of one, as wonderful as you might sound, you'll never be discovered. A beautiful voice is a gift from God and should be shared. Chase your dreams with every fiber inside you.

(254.)

It's hard to achieve and sustain happiness when your happiness depends on other people being happy. It's hard to win when you have to bet on other people.

(255.)

Sometimes the best sound in the world is complete silence; so quiet you can hear yourself think.

(256.)

If you'll die to save your mother; die to save your child, but won't die to save your wife; you married the wrong woman.

(257.)

Only a cheater will cheat on you; only a liar will lie to you; only a thief will steal from you; only a monster will put his hands on you; only a King will treat you like a Queen.

(258.)

I often find myself reminiscing on the black and white days; when man didn't have 10 percent of the tools we have today and created monuments that have stood the test of time. Despite man's greatest accomplishments, travelling to the Moon and back; one thing he can't figure out is how to live in peace.

(259.)

Every now and then I go dark, shut down everything; family, friends, TV, and computer. Sometimes you got to step back and take a look at yourself. If you don't like what you see, it's time to make changes.

(260.)

Hard economic times have a way of revealing one's true worth. Only a criminal will result to crimes in times of need. Be mindful, the worse possible situation on the streets, is better than the best possible situation in prison. As long as you have your health and freedom you have opportunity.

(261.)

I bear witness it's only by the mercy of God I'm still standing, still breathing to enjoy another day in the company of my loved ones. I testify it's only by the power of prayer I'm able to pursue and conquer what my heart desires. For the dreams I have yet to fulfilled, the hurdles I have yet to leap. I embrace my faith and patiently waits for the moment God sees fit to make my life complete.

The End!

www.ingramcontent.com/pod-product-compliance
Lightning Source LLC
Chambersburg PA
CBHW070247100426
42743CB00011B/2173